Jubilee Worldwide!

Youssef Khalim

DEDICATION

To: Larisa Khalim (The real or ideal soul mate: inspiration)

Tonya Tracy Khalim and

Runako Soyini Khalim, (my most beloved daughters)

Mother and Grandmother and Great-grandmother, (my most
beloved maternal biological ancestors, and spiritual antecedents)

M. A. Garvey (one of my 7 M's: my role models)

Youssef Khalim II; III (my most beloved sons)

Father and Grandfather and Great-grandfather, (my most beloved
paternal biological ancestors, and spiritual antecedents)

To: The Forerunners and Reincarnation sources (beloved
biological ancestors and spiritual antecedents), and

The Almighty (our Spiritual Father), from whence we come.

CONTENTS

ACKNOWLEDGMENTS

To: The Forerunners and Reincarnation sources (beloved biological ancestors and spiritual antecedents), and

The Almighty (our Spiritual Father), from whence we come.

1 JUBILEE WORLDWIDE! AFTER THE 2012 ELECTION

Each individual (body) has two each feet, legs, arms, and hands. To sustain our body we need adequate food, clothing, and shelter. Historically, we needed land and its bounty to provide for our needs.

In these times most of us are separated from the land we'd require to cultivate and exploit – to live off the land. We live in a world removed – where society lives by an unwritten social and economic contract that requires us to work at a job for pay as an employer or employee. With this pay, we can purchase the products and services we need.

Modern technology, robotics, and machines have made much of the work previously done by humans a thing of the past. Production is so high and efficient that the labor force participation rate today is at 63.5 percent in the USA: a 31-year low.

When I was in the US Air Force, we all had jobs. In the Amish community, everyone has a job. When I attended Sunday school, we each had a job, a role. Among the early Christians, each individual had a role, a job. When we were back on the land, we all had jobs. We are now about 12-years into the Second Coming: We will all have jobs.

Thomas Jefferson said that whenever government becomes a tyrannical despot, depriving you of life, liberty, and the pursuit of happiness, it is your right; it is your duty to alter or abolish it.

The US Supreme Court is an albatross around the neck, a monkey on the backs of the American people. It is an intolerable tyrannical monstrosity. Citizens United is the last straw.

The US Congress, especially the Republican/Tea Party faction is in active insurrection and sabotage against the American economy, the President, and the people. They pledge allegiance to Grover Norquist, the NRA, & Wall Street. They show more fidelity and loyalty to the State of Israel than the USA – which *is* Israel.

The US Supreme Court and the faction of the US Congress in active revolt against the USA show that those institutions must be altered or abolished.

Each individual (body) needs just so much to insure its well-being, safety, and security. Beyond that, greed enters in. Acts 2: 44-45 says, "And all that believed were together, and had all things common; And sold their possessions and goods, and parted them to all *men*, as every man had need."

Acts 4:32, 35 says, "And the multitude of them that believed were of one heart and of one soul: neither said any *of them* that ought of the things which he possessed was his own; but they had all things common. And laid them down at the apostles' feet: and distribution was made unto every man according as he had need."

Billionaires and the super-rich are taking over the USA government and US institutions, and monopolizing US and world resources. They must be neutralized and quarantined as necessary.

Thomas Jefferson, who is the reincarnation of Jacob, father of the 12-boys whose offspring became known as Israel, told you what you must do. And I'm back again, affirming what he said.

Jubilee: Leviticus 25:8-13 says, "And thou shall number 7 Sabbaths of years unto thee, 7 times 7 years; and the space of 7 Sabbaths of years shall be unto thee 40 and 9 years. Then shalt thou cause the trumpet of the Jubilee to sound on the 10th day of the 7th month, in the Day of Atonement shall ye make the trumpet sound throughout the land. And ye shall hallow the fiftieth year, and proclaim liberty throughout all the land unto all the inhabitants thereof: it shall be a Jubilee unto you. And ye shall return every man unto his possession, and ye shall return every man unto his family."

After the 2012 election, we will begin to implement Jubilee Worldwide!

The USA National Debt is now over $16 Trillion

Consider how the USA national debt increased from the time of President Jimmy Carter:

a) It was about **$994 billion** when Jimmy Carter left office;

b) It was about **$2.867 trillion** when Ronald Reagan left office;

c) It was about **$4.351 trillion** when H. W. Bush left office;

d) It was about **$5.638 trillion** when Bill Clinton left office;

e) It was about **$10.7 trillion in December, 2008** (when the economy was near the beginning of its recent downward spiral);

f) It is over $16 trillion today, in part due to two wars, drug benefits, and tax cuts.

Many governments are flirting with economic disaster at the national, state, and local levels. This is also true with respect to individuals, businesses, etc. Therefore, the Lord our God has made provision for all in the *Law of Jubilee*:

"Jubilee will cancel (reset to zero or make current) all debt, including federal (national), state, local, business, farm, individual, student, family, and international. So, all countries, like the USA, Russia, Greece, Poland, Mexico, Nigeria, Brazil, Zaire, Canada, etc. become completely free of debt." ***Jubilee could be implemented over a period of 5-years, and does not have to be completed all at once.***

Jubilee, Worldwide is an economic and social blueprint for constructing parts of the New Millennium.

2 WHAT IS JUBILEE?

Jubilee is privatization.

It is a prelude to creating and implementing the Millennium. It is a process of creating balance and harmony. For those of the Judeo-Christian-Islamic Tradition, it is The Law of God as handed down through Moses, and modified, especially, by Major Prophets like Jesus and Muhammad. And, it is part of the process of completing that tradition, which we call the "Cycle of Judaism."

For others, it may be seen as The Law of Nature, for one aspect of nature is to operate in cycles, and periodically, or at times, to obtain a balance, or equilibrium. See Leviticus 25:8-13.

The earth is the Lord's and the fullness thereof. 1 Corinthians 10:26 (i.e. "the earth is the Lord's, and everything in it"). *Note: We are about 12-years into the Millennium, also called the Second Coming, the Judgment, and/or the Resurrection.*

So, we will share our knowledge, skills, patents, work, etc. with the world because we are true Muslims, and real Christians, and real Jews.
Jews, Christians, and Muslims, together, may build a Second Solomon Temple somewhere in the midland, in the heartland of the USA.

Amnesty will prevail wherever possible. We will also unclog the local and other courts. And we will educate, rehabilitate, or eliminate individuals, as necessary.

We must be about Our Father's Business of creating The Real New World Order. And that is about food, clothing, shelter, housing, education, health care, and privacy, as a primary right. And the right of all people to have their God-given rights shall not be infringed upon.

Everyone will work or contribute. Every able-bodied person will produce something or provide a service.

Businesses will abide by the same laws as the rest of society. If businesses are caught violating the laws, the RICO statues will apply to their criminal activities, and they will be given to more worthy owners. Always, the golden rule will apply.

The system will be administered fairly!

Jubilee could be implemented over a period of 4 to 5-years, and does not have to be implemented all at once.

4

Precedents to Jubilee Worldwide

1. The Emancipation Proclamation

2. The Louisiana Purchase

3. The colonization/acquisition of the United States, North, Central, and South America

4. The lack of remuneration to former slaves "emancipated" by Abraham Lincoln

5. The lack of remuneration to slave-owning individuals who lost their "assets" due to the Emancipation and Civil War

6. Reparations payments to the state of Israel

7. Reparations payments to Japanese Americans who were wrongfully incarcerated in the USA

8. Infrastructure, employment, and construction programs (of the CCC and the WPA) under President Franklin D. Roosevelt

Also, See:

Acts 2:44 (Consider the "Community" references below from Acts: 2: 44-45 and 4: 32, 35)

[44] And all that believed were together, and had all things common;
[45] And sold their possessions and goods, and **parted them to all men, as every man had need.**

Acts 4:32

[32] And the multitude of them that believed were of one heart and of one soul: neither said any of them that ought of the things which he possessed was his own; but they had all things common.
[35] **And laid them down at the apostles' feet: and distribution was made unto every man according as he had need.**

The USA is Israel

1. Thomas Jefferson is the reincarnation of Jacob, father of *the* renowned 12-boys that became known as Israel.

2. Prophet Muhammad is the reincarnation of Moses. This *is* no joke, and it was presented to me as an almost obvious fact.

3. President Barack Obama is the reincarnation of President Abraham Lincoln. On a subconscious level, you already know this. Speakers and writers "compare" Obama to Lincoln, over and over – for good reason. Obama reminds them of Lincoln – because he is Lincoln. Just as Lincoln sought to unite America, so does Obama. But half of America (the core are the children of same Southerners) fight against him, and subvert, undermine, and sabotage the economic, social, and political fabric of the USA: treason. How ironic, since Obama, as Lincoln, "created" the Republican Party – where these traitors now reside.

Daniel 4:21 says, "The most high God ruled in the kingdom of men, and that he appointeth over it whomsoever he will."

Daniel 5:25 says, "The most High ruleth in the kingdom of men, and giveth it to whomsoever he will."

We are about 12-years into The Second Coming (The Bible says it lasts for 1000 years.)
   The old paradigms are obsolete: labor, work, politics, government, the Nation-State, pseudo-religions, lack of integrity, the multinational corporation structure, the current economic system, the corrupt, obscene social system, tribalism, bigotry, the war-mongering military-industrial complex, etc.
   The Second Coming can be ascertained and verified using the 1260-year prophecies, sometimes given as *42 months* (Daniel 7:25, 12:7, Revelation 11:2, 11:3, 12:6, 12:14, 13:5), the **2300-year prophecy** (Daniel 8:14, 9:24-27), the **1335-year prophecy** of Daniel 12:12, the **2520-year prophecy** (Daniel 4:15-16, 23, 25, 32), the *42 kings vs. 42 presidents*, in Matthew and Luke, the **1-8 Empires** indicator in Rev. 17:11, plus historical events. It started during the Clinton Administration.

So, The Second Coming is a number of things:

- It is a time when science, technology, and innovation create the conditions for "heaven on earth."
- It is a time when those conditions and individuals in opposition to truth, justice, caring, sharing, and openness, and privacy will not exist on earth.
- It is the beginning of The Millennium, spoken of in the Bible.

- It is the time of The First Resurrection. See Revelation 20.
- It is the time of The Judgment, and The Resurrection, spoken of in The Holy Qur'an.
- It is a time when integrity and truth will be rigorous not only in business, science, architecture, and technology, but also in religion, social relations, spiritual matters, economics, and social policy.

Justice and fairness will be integral components, along with truth and integrity.

- The Second Coming is like having brunch at *a buffet*: You can have all that you can consume, all you need, and you are free to have what you want. But you have to pay an entry fee. And the entry fee is quite reasonable. And everyone will participate in a just and fair manner, creating, building, caring, and sharing.

Let's implement Jubilee Worldwide and Strengthen the Second Coming!

3 WHEN IS JUBILEE?

Jubilee will occur as soon as legislation is enacted to accomplish it – or a mass movement facilitates it. We ask that the113th Congress enact it. We are starting a Jubilee Party, of people of the United States (and elsewhere), to democratically enact a form of Jubilee in the USA and worldwide, ASAP.

The present governments (federal, local, etc.) are weak, impotent, worthless, and incompetent; yet they are destructive, wasteful, invasive, and arrogant. They are too often where they should not be. And they are too often not there when you need help. But they are always there, digging in your pocket for money. And they let businesses, especially, run roughshod over the people. These governments are much worse, in many ways, than the government that was overthrown in 1776. In many ways, they are worse than the governments that were overthrown in Eastern Europe, and elsewhere.

In Chicago, for example, right after an April 4th election, the mayor and aldermen conspired to raise the aldermanic salary 36% (to about $75000) and the Mayor's salary by $55,000 to $170,000! Then, they will tell you they are public servants; "for the people," etc.

And in the past, on the national level, Newt Gingrich, the guru of family values and morality, said he opposed meaningfully raising the minimum wage above $4.25 per hour ($170 per week. $8840 per year). (So, here you have it- $8,840 vs. $170,000. And who really works, and produces something of value?)

That Newt, and the other crooks, should be made to live on the wage they advocate for other people! And Newt could show that he's not a phony and live on minimum wage voluntarily.

Anyway, at the local level, at the national level, you have these snakes that rule over society, in business, in government, and elsewhere. Now, all of them are not devils. But, as an institution on the various levels, they are enemies of the people. They suck the blood of the people. They are oppressors. They violate the first principle of morality - which is to treat others like they want to be treated. And they should be retired!

Anyway, their hold on society, at all levels should be removed immediately. Jubilee will accomplish that. So, we want Jubilee now. Because, if this is a government of the people, by the people, for the people, we must replace it with something better. And anyway, real people (not devils) are better than that. People are much better than what this society and this government are.

4 WHO WILL IMPLEMENT JUBILEE?

Jubilee will be implemented by the same types, and the same forces as was the revolution in India (led by Gandhi), the Abolitionist Movement in the USA, or the Civil Rights Movement in the USA:

The religious community and the intelligencia will execute Jubilee, and lead the movement toward bartering, and they will create the real New World Order.

Where you find higher spiritual development, intelligence, initiative, dedication to God and man, truthfulness and courage, and unselfishness in one individual, like Gandhi, Martin Luther King Jr., Moses, Jesus, Muhammad, etc.; these will be the types in the leadership (in the flesh, or in the spirit) who will spearhead:

1) The completion of the Cycle of Judaism

2) The Spiritual Revolution, so that we will understand again that, as with our Father, spirit (or soul) is the utmost nature of our being. For, we are all created like Him. And that God is One, and that only in Unity can there be unity with God.

3) The Second Coming. For the Second Coming is in some ways like the First. It is knowledge (light, intelligence) of material and spiritual matters. It is putting these into the proper perspective. BUT THE SECOND COMING IS ALSO PART OF THE JUDGMENT, for the devils will be sent to hell.

4). And those who do not join this Spiritual Movement, which creates the conditions in our new home, The Millennium (of bartering, security, justice, privacy, and respect, caring and sharing) are not worthy to enter into it.

We will be going to a society of God and His people, by God and His people, for the Glory of God and His Creation. And that is the "after."

Look at what we have now, the "before." The USA economy and the Fed's role in it creates an unnatural and pathological condition similar to bulimia: overeating (inflation) and then self-induced vomiting, or the taking of laxatives to rid the body of food (recession or depression).

The Fed's preoccupation with inflation is like an obsessive concern with thinness and weight loss. And serious nutritional deficiencies, metabolic imbalance, even heart disorders can be created. The economy lurches forward, runs backwards,

- Becomes more and more efficient

- Reduces more and more, real wages

- Creates more and more insecurity

- Creates more and more crime

- Builds more and more jails

- Raises more and more taxes

- AND BECOMES MORE AND MORE INSANE (AND SATANIC)

Meanwhile, some CEO'S (just like a cancer) get 25 to 1400 times the pay of the average worker. Many Athletes and entertainers receive similar pay. And athletes, basically, produce nothing (except, maybe, momentary enjoyment, or distraction, away from the real world).

Also, entertainers often help pollute the society and undermine correct values. Just listen to their mouths.

Also, many elements, or functions of the society are like lupus. They turn on society. This can be found in the government, business, illegal and legal drug dealing, religious groups, etc. There is official government gambling, unfunded mandates (federal, state, local), and the practice of processing and warehousing criminals to create jobs.

Business, generally, opposes raising the minimum wage(s) to a living wage. And business is exempt from many laws (like fraud, lying, etc.) that the rest of society may be heavily penalized for violating.

Many religious groups fleece their members and do not help members develop both intellectually and spiritually.

Conversely, the government, and the leadership in the society must perform as facilitators and coordinators. And they must be those who see society as one whole body, which cares about, and shares with all its component parts.

For, the heart and mind (brain), pituitary, pineal, thyroid, parathyroids, lungs, liver, gonads, or ovaries, kidneys, ears, eyes see, and work together in healthy individuals. And nutrition is distributed to all the cells of the body.

There is no redlining, or denial of nutrition to the left arm. The right hand does not embargo its thumb by cutting off circulation to it. Leucocytes do not attack cells because they have melanin. And the latter does not despise the leucocytes because they lack color.

The lungs do not mine (or enslave) the heart. The DNA pairs know their place, and do not separate from their twin, but rather, work cooperatively, and complement. And the healthy (united) society results. Because only in unity can there be unity with God.

By the way, religious groups, especially should understand: During the time of Jesus, there were Essenes, and Zealots, Pharisees, Sadducees (materialists), scribes (media), etc., and these groups were very similar to what we have today.

For, many of today's groups think their own group, or sect is the closer version of society or religious correctness. At least one significant group does not vote. At least one has blatant and outrageous lies concerning the origin of racial difference.

To the first group: Go back and review the life of Jeremiah, Daniel, Jesus, et.al. Did they branch off and form their own individual groups away from the people, away from the body of God's people? When you overly separate yourself from the body, you may separate yourself from God's plans for the whole body politic.

There is a time when we need to be a part of the whole body. Maybe the brain, maybe the heart. Maybe the feet, or ears. And when you splinter off, you may very well be splintering off from God's purpose and God's plan.

See with your individual eyes. Think with your individual mind. Feel with your individual heart and emotions. There is a time coming when your vote will count because God counts on you. And you count. Many are called but most are not chosen because they choose to be too busy to be prepared by Him to do what He wants. And many busy bodies are so caught up in their own organization, their own sect, and their own clique- that they are too busy for God.

Can He count on you when He may want to reach you to have you consider thinking for yourself, in the knowledge that you will be judged as an individual?

If the mind is not closely in touch and in tune with the body, it may put the body in harm's way. Or, conversely, it could save the body. Consider what you do, for the time is at hand.

And to the latter group: Truth should be one of the first considerations in spiritual matters-in all matters. We must always be true to ourselves. Lies are not of God, but of the devil. And again, we all must think for ourselves. Remember, we are all one body, in God. And God is One. Unity is key. Again, we all count.

11

5 NOW LET ME GET THIS STRAIGHT –
ABOUT BARTERING

Under the current economic system in the USA, the citizens are taught that they have free enterprise, free trade, competition, equal opportunity for all, etc.

The Federal Reserve System (the FED) monitors the money supply, wages, employment, house and real estate construction and sales, productivity, inflation, efficiency, the stock market, farming conditions, factory capacity utilization, etc.

Now, you and I know that it would be desirable (even necessary) for an individual, each individual, in fact, to be gainfully employed, or to be contributing to our society. That is because you have to eat, provide housing, buy clothes, pay for utilities, etc.,

So, let me get this straight. When you actually start getting remotely close to real full employment, that is bad news for the FED, and they may raise interest rates, and the cost of a mortgage may go up by, say, $60, or $200 (if it is flexible). And businesses may go under because they cannot borrow, at the higher rates. And if they borrow, they have to add the higher cost of borrowing to their products, which is inflationary.

And housing construction, and sales, may slow to a trickle. And people will be hard pressed to afford the higher rate mortgages. And the sale of a number of items will slow, so that businesses will start to lay off workers. And this will make the FED happy, and now they may lower rates.

And the whole process is insanity and satanic! And this is something thought up, and administered by the devil.

But remember now, we have free trade, free enterprise, competition, and above all, a free society. And the so-called capitalists will tell you about the awful central planners and command economies. Those devils should look in the mirror.

What the FED does is idiotic, and it shows that the economic system is idiotic and evil. It is like grabbing a man by the balls and saying, "You are free to go wherever you please. You are free, you are free, you are free." You can say freedom forever. But, you just watch and see how far he is free to go!

So, let's get this straight:

Only bartering will free the people and free the society.

Now, farmers often do not want a bumper crop, because it may drive down prices.

So, let me get this straight.... They want to limit supplies to boost prices, so we, the consumers, will have to pay more. And we just saw that employers (and the FED) want, even engineer: excess employees to depress wages.

COULD THAT POSSIBLY BE REAL?

Let me get this straight. You have this Easter egg hunt involving four children. You tie #4 up (and you make him work for you, for free) while the other three find and claims 90% of the eggs. Then, you let the 4th one join in the hunt. You take #4 and put him and his offspring in a Bantustan for a few generations. You redline the Bantustan. You embargo it. You deny credit to the inhabitants while it is offered to the three others. You wage psychological warfare against the inhabitants.

Then, there is a process to redress some of the past inequities, (and to offer some opportunity to the descendants of #4), but a certain percentage of the offspring of the three call that reverse discrimination.

So, don't be surprised if people who go to hell because of their own actions and inactions say that God is unfair, unkind, and unjust.

Let me get this straight. I borrow money (and I have to pay it back, with interest). I then invest it in a corporation. They give me my money back and pay me interest on the principal. Then, I notice (for example) that a loaf of bread was about $.15 (in about 1960). And I recently saw a loaf of bread that sells for well over $2.00.

Now, I wonder where the FED has been over the last 35 years when just about everything has at least tripled or quadrupled in price. And isn't it apparent that the use and misuse of interest is inherent in the system, and automatically drives up the price of everything.

Let me get this straight. I work and create a product to export. The import country has few factories, so many of their workers come to this country and they take a job (at depressed wages) because there is an excess of workers. Then, their family and relatives come. And now the FED is really elated.

Then, all Americans have to work really, really hard because there are few factories where the people who want work are. And they keep coming here. And our government is constantly giving billions to Israel, Egypt, NATO, etc.

And the USA workers have to work more and more. And it becomes patently clear to you that if you gave other workers, (other countries) the patents (and/or knowhow), and helped them build the factory, you would have more time to be a better human being, and think of better ways to help put this country out of its misery.

But there will be better days with bartering. We will have better days. And believe me, everyone will help produce the things we want and need.

6 DOES BARTERING WORK?

Bartering was the method of trade used greatly from about 3100 B.C. to about 676 B.C. in Egypt. It was used in Kush. It was used greatly in ancient Israel (for many hundreds of years). It was greatly used in the Muslim Empires for many hundreds of years. In fact, our system *is* supposed to be a kind of barter system. But, it is controlled by (let us be kind and say) people who don't have our best interests at heart.

People who speculate, manipulate, exploit, and enslave have too much control over it. It is a paper money system and the way it operates is like driving your car with one foot constantly on the brake and one foot constantly on the accelerator, but favoring one at any given time.

The kind of system we have is partly realized by noting that a Mr. Soros earned a billion dollars in one day, speculating on the British Pound, years ago.

Conversely, One example of a barter system would be a family of two adults, two boys, and one girl. One boy will cut the grass. One will empty the trash, walk the dog. The girl will wash the dishes. Mom will cook, wash. Maybe she will also have a job. Dad will vacuum; water the grass. Mom will analyze and pay the bills. Everyone has something to do. They do not necessarily charge money for their services, or the goods they produce and provide. They share in what has to be done.

One child is not segregated and ostracized, or discriminated against.. No child is denied love, or nourishment. There is no price put on a hug, or kiss, or affection, or a kind word. There is mutual support. There is, ideally, unity of purpose.

In so-called primitive societies, the system of barter works in a similar manner.

- So, in our new society, none of our children (citizens) will use food stamps, for example, because you should not treat your children differently.

- Major factories may become owned, first, by the employees and then by the public. Those who have a mind and a heart will work this out.

- Much privatization may occur, but remember, students, (all of us) will get all the education that we can consume.

And, for example, teachers will teach, full of security, knowing that all of their needs will be met.

Part of what should be taught and learned is that you cannot put a price on everything. For, it is like putting a tariff on each and every type and quantity of nutrition as it moves through the structures, organs, and cells of the body. It deforms, then, destroys the body. And this is true for the body politic also. Again, we must focus on providing work, and nutrition to the whole body.

The "interest" system "jacks up" the price of everything. If you compare things to a ladder, then, they are often moved up beyond the reach of even those who produce the "things." And those who fall off the economic ladder find it ever more difficult to climb back on. For, prices are ever rising on things.

Again, we must focus on providing work, and nutrition to the whole body.

Regarding Antitrust legislation, most must be removed. For, again, it is like saying to the liver, or heart, or lungs, or brain, respectively, "We don't trust you to do your job, so let's get some competition in there to compete against you."

We must face the fact that much of the justice system itself is unjust, unfair, and immoral. Why do federal and Supreme Court judges have well paying, lifetime employment (security), "shooting-the breeze," while most of the rest of their fellow citizens can get a pink slip at just about any time? If the status of these individuals brings out the noblest in them, then it will bring out the noblest in everybody.

Also, part-time, or Temporary Employment, is sweeping the country. And that type employment is a practice where a temporary employee (e.g.), may work right alongside a regular employee, (doing the same work), but receive much less in wages, benefits, etc. And the Supreme Court does nothing about this. It reminds me of the approximate 100 years that the Supreme Court was "out to lunch" when African Americans were blatantly and brutally oppressed and denied citizenship rights.

And The Supreme Court has not resolved issues like abortion, discrimination, unemployment, the gang problem, the federal debt problem, the balance of trade problem, etc., partly because *it* is part of the problem.

SO, WE WANT GOD TO JUDGE THE JUDGES, AND RENDER JUDGMENT! And God will give better; we will get things to where they belong.

For with all the efficiencies obtained over the last 50 years, it an easy thing to get all things to the people, if only the will is present. And the obstacles will be removed.

The trumpet of God will sound throughout the land And every man, woman, and child will choose.

And we will witness the most surprising events in human history, for some.

For, we indeed will overcome!

Then, Builders will build.

Teachers will teach.

The bells will chime as He comes near.

And singers will sing.

The bells will toll and ring.

Then, we will sing:

"Free at last
Free at last
Thank God, Almighty
We're free, at last."

7 ISSUES

Did you know?

- 1/5 of the children of the USA go hungry

- In 1993, it was said that 37 million citizens had no health insurance

- About 5.5% unemployment is considered full employment

- About 13.5% of GDP goes for health care compared to about 7.5% in 1972.

- The USA prison population doubled in the 1980's

- The cost of keeping an individual in jail is over $11,000, or $212 weekly

- Citizens spent 3.25 times more of their annual income on taxes in 1990 compared to 1929.

- Real earnings have actually fallen 11.2% since 1970

- In 1993, it was estimated that 17 million persons were unemployed or under- employed

- In 1990, total government employment was about 19.3 million persons, or about 14.8% of the labor force

- Between 1980 and 1990, the number of farms fell from 2.4 million to 2.1 million

- 1.2 million manufacturing jobs were lost in the 1980's

- Oil imports account for over 50% of domestic needs

- In 1990, interest on the national debt was $264.9 billion, or 21.2% of federal expenditures

- The federal debt will increase about $1 trillion during Clinton's term. Etc.

So, many indicators show a government and a society in decay, collapse, and/or out of control.

FDR would never have tolerated the growth of gangs, the drug problem, the stupidity that exists regarding the issue of abortion, the issue of gun control, imbalance of trade, antitrust, etc.

The problem of gangs will be solved with testing, (screening) work (employment), reeducation, rehabilitation, or elimination. Period. And Malcom X was such an rehabilitated individual whose life demonstrates that rehabilitation works.

The drug problem will be solved by first, creating a society where what is natural is seen as desirable, and the incentive for drugs is reduced or eliminated. Again, reeducation and rehabilitation is key. The body is the temple of the living God, and people will be taught that first. And God will eliminate what is really unfit for society. Remember, God has promised to send devils to hell.

The first thing that should be said about abortion is that sometimes, (most often, in fact) people should keep their nose out of other people's business.

Defective people do not respect other people's privacy and space. And, generally, they're not too bright.

While we should respect all life, we are never to impose our will on others, except to deter them from encroaching on our own space and individuality.

When the individual breathes the breathe of life into the body (at birth), he then becomes a living soul.

And some people are not bright enough to understand the fundamentals. They would force a possibly defective person to bring a child into the world, and basically, they do nothing (cannot do anything substantial) to make the world a better place, a workable place. They don't seem to realize that like begets like.

But, devils like to force their will on others, and they guard their own privacy like greedy, hungry animals eating bloody, red meat. "We will do what?" Test, educate, rehabilitate or eliminate.

Regarding the gun issue, some of the people want their guns because they are afraid of the government, or society. Never mind the fact of being out-gunned by the government. Many of them have seen the government up close, and have been a part of the government's evil deeds. And many of them have been a part of the government's efforts in doing bad (wrong) things to people. No wonder they are fearful. And the unjust will always reap what they sow. So, give a pacifier to a baby, and leave a gun to the gun lovers. Leave them alone.

Higher-level people realize truth is more potent than pistols. And God is certainly on the side of the righteous. His servants are some of His weapons. His weapons are best. And we do not need weapons.

Regarding trade, as we said earlier, an imbalance of trade can never exist in bartering, because bartering is exchange.

And finally, antitrust legislation makes no sense in our new world. Food, clothing, shelter, education, health care, etc., are the focus.

We will create external and internal security. The reassessment of the military's mission and its budget must get underway immediately. We will consider using the military like King David, Eisenhower, Truman, FDR, Moses, Joshua, or Muhammad did.

"And the earth will be full of the knowledge of the Lord, as the waters cover the sea... for the Lord has set His hand again the second time to recover the remnant of His people, which shall be left, from Assyria, and from Egypt, and from Pathros, and from Cush, and from Elam, and from Hamath, and from the islands of the sea." Isaiah 11: 9, 11.

8 WHAT'S THE PROBLEM?

It is now 7/03/2006. I am inserting this small section into *Jubilee Worldwide* today to emphasize what I see as continuing or escalating problems.

The problems that the world (and its people face) include, or are caused by:

- Deficient culture (a defective worldview)
- Mis-education
- Lack of scientific and technical education
- An inability to think logically, rationally
- Lack of opportunity
- Discrimination
- Injustice
- Lack of integrity in the people themselves and/or others
- Anti-intellectualism
- Warmongering by the USA and "Israel" They act like Rome, Greece.
- Corrupt Puppet Regimes set-up and/or maintained by the 8th World Power
- Greed, selfishness, envy
- Huge defects in the Economic System
- Psychological Warfare waged against some (like African Americans)
- The (Illegal) Drug Problem
- The Gang problem
- The Prison System
- Maybe 60% (or more) of the US Congress in the pocket of (or executing the will of) the "Israeli Lobby"
- The US voters somehow "electing" a regime like the Bush regime. What does that say about so-called Democracy?
- Etc.

Now, some possible solutions:

The problems of miseducation and a defective worldview can be fixed by real education, truth, and openness. I have addressed many of the other issues elsewhere in this book. The solutions to many of the problems are obvious. To partially compensate African Americans for the centuries of prohibition from education, miseducation, discrimination, oppression and Psychological Warfare waged against them, we propose extending massive and comprehensive (real) education to them. Teach them about the culture and architecture of Karnak, Luxor, Egypt, Ethiopia, Nigeria, Mali, "Ghana," Kush, Europe, India, Yemen, and other places.

The culture here was erased, wiped-out. In the void, devils placed much that is garbage, mis-education, lies, wrong thoughts, bad examples. Let's have culture improvement here, starting with a better religion.

Re-establish the Caliphate? Actually, the reestablished Caliphate will be synonymous with "religion" in the Millennium.

Because Prophet Muhammad said, in:

9:33 It is He Who has sent His Messenger with guidance and the religion of truth (Islâm), that He may **make it to prevail over all religions** even though the Mushrikûn (polytheists, pagans, idolaters, disbelievers in the Oneness of Allâh) hate it.

In 48:28, he said: He it is Who has sent His Messenger with guidance and the religion of truth, that He may make it **prevail over all religions.** And All-Sufficient is Allâh as a Witness.

And in 61:9, he said: He it is Who has sent His Messenger with guidance and the religion of truth to **make it prevail over all religions** even though the Mushrikûn disbelievers hate it.

I believe Prophet Muhammad is right!

Teach them about religions: Tell them how life really works. Give them land! Give them Africa (United)!

Next, Give them a positive, constructive worldview. Tell them that George Washington Carver, Isaac Newton, and Albert Einstein are their "new" role models. Then watch the African American Community blossom! Watch Africa become a gem - and the USA, heaven-on earth!

Last week I noticed that Bill Gates (of Microsoft) and Warren Buffet were going to give away (or contribute) huge sums (billions of dollars) to worthwhile causes and/or charitable organizations.

I thought: "Hmmmm. Is that a sign of the times?" Could this be part of what we want with Jubilee?"

Of course, "Bono" and others are addressing the problem of "freeing" some countries from crippling debt. Could this also be a sign of the times?

I conceived of the "forgive all debt" in 1992, which forms the basis of this book. In 1993, I even had a rhyming slogan that embodied that idea.

"Jubilee in '93!" I said.

It has been interesting to see that idea advocated, developed, and implemented by some churches, in some instances, and in some places.

Now, let's do a massive and comprehensive *Jubilee Worldwide*!

9 GEORGE BUSH SAID THE US CURRENCY IS BOGUS

George W. Bush once said the Treasury Bill debt, money owed to The Social Security Administration, to other individuals, businesses, and governments was not real money.

He implied that it would not be repaid.

He is partly right. Some of that money may never be repaid. But I think he hit on something that we should think about. A Currency System, as opposed to a Money System, seems to have a built-in mechanism that kills it.

In the USA, it may be a slow death. A building worth $20,000.00 in 1969 may be worth $500,000.00 today - same building. A loaf of bread costing $0.15 in 1961 will cost over $2.00 today. And this process of devaluation (or inflation) accounts for most of that "change in value."

When you have a Currency System - and it is racist, discriminatory, unfair, and "bogus," its days are numbered.

We need *fair* bartering, and we should consider how the matter of "interest" is handled in Islam, and in the Law of Moses.

10 THINGS THAT MAKE MY BLOOD BOIL: MONSTERS

I went by the Jewel Food Store over by Ashland Blvd. and Roosevelt Rd. in Chicago last night (7/4/2006) starting at about 12:00 AM (this morning).

I did my shopping and was waiting in line behind two young guys, a young woman, and a child of about 2 years-old. By now it was about 12:40 AM.

The child was seated in the grocery cart, and he fell asleep. So he was sleeping, sitting-up. His head would careen to the left. He would jump, with a start! But he would not wake up. Then, he would careen for- wards, or backwards, or to the right - same reaction, over, and over, and over!

The woman was reading a magazine. The guys were talking among themselves. They paid no attention to this young child - and his misery.

First, I said something to one of the guys about the baby. He said, "OK, I know." Later, the young child careened so far to the left or forward, that I caught his head.

Then, one of the guys said, in so many words, "I got the situation under control!" His tone said, "Mind your own business!"

My blood boiled! How could any human being be so calloused, actually cruel - to a two-year-old child. He was such a lovely child.

This group of people looked like African Americans, but they are not really African American. They are something that this society has created. And they are very scary, because they lack basic human qualities.

These creations are also the types that "enabled" the establishment of the evil, satanic, lying, corrupt, and communistic organizations like the *Department of Children and Family Services* (DCFS) in Illinois.

This group of people also demonstrate what over 400 years of oppression, dehumanization, psychological warfare, and discrimination can do to a people.

Bill Cosby recently commented about this type of people. I think we once called them the Underclass. At any rate, (we, the society) have created a monster. Maybe it is somewhat like a cancer. These people need a lot of "fixing!"

Way back in the seventies, James (my brother), Earl (a friend), Chuck (our cousin), and others used to talk about how bad things were then. That was before Crack Cocaine and other evils ravaged some parts of the African American Community and this country.

I used to say, "We need some form of regimentation, maybe Martial Law" to address some of the problems that existed.

I now believe "Modern Islam" can remedy the problems in America, especially in the African American Community.

God is easy. God is fun! He is Grace. God is a wonderful friend! Modern Islam is the religion of The Millennium, for Muhammad said, "It will prevail over all other religions!" It will co-opt what is essential in Judaism, Christianity, and Orthodox Islam. See *The Resurrection of Noah.* " *See 48:28, 9:33, and 61:9.*

It appears that all of these 3- religions have deviated from their core message and much of what should have been their fundamental tenets. We will fix that, and establish true religion, science, philosophy - and Modern Islam. See 42:13-15.

11 THE BUMS OVER BY DIVISION STREET AND I90/94 IN CHICAGO

Another thing which makes my blood boil is the situation of the Home- less, especially the ones in Wicker Park. You know how we are: "Not in my neighborhood!" We don't want homeless in *our* neighborhood.

Going North on I90/94, when you exit at Division Street, you encounter them under the bridge. About 3 or 4 of them have made "permanent homes" under the bridge. They have their "beds" in their various spaces. Actually, they make "beds" on the concrete pillars, right adjacent to the sidewalk. Then, at times when I drive by, I see them sitting in a nearby chair, or on the concrete pillars. Sometimes, one or more of them are out begging - panhandling.

To me, people are divine, sacred! Many of these beggars, these Home- less, on Division Street, and throughout Chicago (and this country) have lost their way, their human dignity, pride, and their sense of self.

We need to get them off the streets! They are an affront to God! They offend mankind too, because they have sunk far below what is acceptable in our human community.

I believe the society suffers because some of these people "who may be outside" society may be involved in petty vandalism, damage to property, and petty theft.

Too frequently, I will give money to the needy and people in distress. Just yesterday (7/7/2006), I gave $10.00 to a guy who said he needed money to get somewhere. (This was over by Wallace's Catfish Corner, at Madison Street and California). Maybe he needed to get home or "to his job." he said he was recently released from jail or prison.

Some people have been devastated by our society, our Prison System, our idiotic Drug Laws, and our social, economic, and political system!

We need to fix a lot of intolerable conditions.

12 PROPHET MUHAMMAD IS THE REINCARNATION OF MOSES

By now you know about the vision I had about the Prophet Muhammad on 5/2/2000.

Here is something I have not told you. Certain visions happen at a level of consciousness, a level of existence, that could not (does not) co-exist with untruth, lies, falsehood, injustice, indecency! See? It's a "location" or condition where the qualities of negativity and "Antichrist" cannot exist. Go look at some of my most intense visions. Look at the one involving Moses/Muhammad. Look at the "Born Again" Vision.

I once told the Host of Odyssey (on Chicago Public Radio) that some in religion believe that Prophet Muhammad is the reincarnation of Moses. I got a nice chuckle out of her.

Whenever I have gotten to know a person well enough, and I felt comfortable doing it (since 5/2/2000), I have told everyone who would listen: Prophet Muhammad is the reincarnation of Moses.

OK, folks! Now I can show you and the world. Look at the excerpts below: Chapter 2

Note: See below: When mentioning Moses, many verses in the Qur'an address Muhammad as you (Moses).

2:49 And **remember when We delivered you** from Fir'aun's (Pharaoh's) people, who were afflicting you with a horrible torment, killing your sons and sparing your women, and therein was a mighty trial from your Lord.

2:50 And **remember when We separated the sea for you, and saved you,** and drowned Pharaoh's people **while you** were looking on.

2:51 And **remember when We appointed for Moses forty nights**, and in his absence you took the calf for worship, and you were Zâlimûn (polytheists and wrongdoers, etc.)

2:87 And indeed, **We gave Mûsa (Moses) the Book and followed him up with a succession of Messengers.** And We gave 'Iesa (Jesus), the son of Maryam (Mary), clear signs and supported him with Rûh-ul-Qudus Jibrael (Gabriel). Is it that whenever there came to you a Messenger with what you yourselves desired not, you grew arrogant? Some, you disbelieved and some, you killed.

2:98 *"Whoever is an enemy to Allâh, His Angels, His Messengers, Jibrael (Gabriel) and Mikael (Michael), then verily, Allâh is an enemy to the disbelievers."*

2:106 *Whatever verse (revelation) We abrogate or cause to be forgotten, We bring a better one or similar to it.* Know you not that Allâh is able to do all things?

2:108 Or **do you want to ask your Messenger, as Moses was asked before (i.e., show us openly our Lord)** And he who changes Faith for disbelief, verily, he has gone astray from the right way

2:136 Say, "We believe in Allâh and that which has been sent down to us and that which has been sent down to Abraham, Ishmael, Isaac, Jacob, and to the twelve sons of Jacob, and that which has been given to Moses and Jesus, and that which has been given to the Prophets from their Lord. We make no distinction between any of them, and to Him we have submitted."

2:138 **Our religion is the Religion of Allâh and which religion can be better than Allâh's?** And we are His worshipers.

Note: Re: verses below, Moses would have faced toward Jerusalem. Why would a non-Moses face toward Jerusalem?

2:142 The fools among the people will say, **"What has turned them (Muslims) from their prayer direction towards Jerusalem to which they used to face in prayer."** Say, "To Allâh belongs both, east and the West. He guides whom He wills to a Straight Way."

2:143 Thus **We have made you a just nation, that you be witnesses over mankind and the Messenger be a witness over you.** And We made the prayer direction towards Jerusalem, which you used to face, only to test those who followed the Messenger from those who would turn on their heels. Indeed it was great except for those whom Allâh guided. And Allâh would never make your faith (prayers) to be lost. Truly, Allâh is full of kindness, the Most Merciful towards man- kind.

29

2:146 **Those to whom We gave the Scripture (Jews and Christians) recognize him (Muhammad or the Ka'bah at Makkah) as they recognize their sons.** But verily, a party of them conceal the truth while they know it.
2:151 Similarly (to complete My Blessings on you) We have sent among you a Messenger (Muhammad) of your own, reciting to you Our Verses (the Qur'ân) and sanctifying you, and teaching you the Book (the Qur'ân) and the Hikmah (i.e., Sunnah, Islâmic laws and Fiqh - jurisprudence), and teaching you that which you used not to know.

How to Interpret the Qur'an

3:7 It is He Who has sent down to you the Book (this Qur'ân). **In it are verses that are entirely clear, they are the foundations of the Book and those are the** Verses of Al-Ahkâm **(commandments, etc.), Al-Farâ'id (obligatory duties)** and Al- Hudud **(legal laws for the punishment of thieves, adulterers**, etc.)]; and **others not entirely clear.** So as for **those in whose hearts there is a deviation (from the truth) they follow that which is not entirely clear** thereof, seeking Al- Fitnah (polytheism and trials, etc.), and seeking for its hidden meanings, but **none knows its hidden meanings save Allâh. And those who are firmly grounded in knowledge,** say We believe in the book; the whole of it is from our Lord." And **none receive admonition except men of understanding.**

Note: Can any intelligent believer doubt that Muhammad is Moses after I Have Told You So, In Truth, and After reading these Excerpts?

3:31 Say: **"If you love Allâh then follow me, Allâh will love you and forgive you of your sins.** And Allâh is Oft-Forgiving, Most Merciful."
3:33 **Allâh chose Adam, Noah, the family of Abraham, and the family of Moses above the 'Alamîn** (mankind and jinns).
3:34 **Offspring, one of the other,** and Allâh is the All-Hearer, All-Knower.
3:50 And I have come confirming that which was before me of the Taurât (Torah), and to make lawful to you part of what was forbidden to you, and I have come to you with a proof from your Lord. So fear Allâh and obey me.

Note: Below is a verse which helps validate our belief that Jesus is the Reincarnation of Adam. See the Bible for additional validation.

3:58 Verily, the likeness of Jesus before Allâh is the like- ness of Adam. He created him from dust, then (He) said to him: "Be!" - and he was.

Note: How could verses 3:67 and 3:69 be true if Muhammad is not Moses?

3:67 Indicates That The Colonial State of Israel Cannot (Continue to) Exist

3:67 **Verily, among mankind those who are nearest to Ibrâhim (Abraham) are those who followed him, and this Prophet (Muhammad), and those who believe.** And Allâh is the Walî (Protector and Helper) of the believers.

3:67 **Verily, among mankind those who are nearest to Ibrâhim (Abraham) are those who followed him, and this Prophet (Muhammad), and those who believe.** And Allâh is the Walî (Protector and Helper) of the believers.
3:69 O people of the Scripture!: "**Why do you disbelieve in the verses about Prophet Muhammad present in the Torah and the Gospel** while you bear witness to their truth."

Chapter 4
4:153 The people of the Scripture (Jews) ask you to cause a book to descend upon them from heaven. Indeed **they asked Mûsa (Moses) for even greater than that, when they said: "Show us Allâh in public,"** but they were struck with thunder clap and lightning for their wickedness. Then they worshipped the calf even after clear proofs, evidences, and signs had come to them. (Even) so We forgave them. And We gave Mûsa (Moses) a clear proof of authority.

4:159 And **there is none of the people of the Scripture (Jews and Christians), but must believe in Jesus, before a Jew's or a Christian's death.** And on the Day of Resurrection, he will be a witness against them.

4:162 But those among them who are well-grounded in knowledge, and the believers, believe in what has been sent down to you and what was sent down before you, and those who perform As–Salât (Iqâmat-as-Salât), and give Zakât and believe in Allâh and in the Last Day, it is they to whom We shall give a great reward.

Note: Why is Moses not mentioned in verse 4:163? The logical answer is because Muhammad is Moses, reincarnated.

4:163 Verily, **We have inspired you as We inspired Nûh (Noah) and the Prophets after him; We also inspired Abraham, Ishmael, Isaac, Jacob,** and the twelve sons of Jacob, Jesus, Ayub (Job), Yûnus (Jonah), Hârûn (Aaron), and Sulaimân (Solomon), and to Dawûd (David) We gave the Zabûr (Psalms). 4:164 And Messengers We have mentioned to you before, and Messengers We have not mentioned to you, - and **to Mûsa (Moses) Allâh spoke directly.**

Chapter 5
5:45 And **We prescribed to them in it that life is for life, and eye for eye, and nose for nose, and ear for ear, and tooth for tooth, and for wounds retaliation.** But whoso forgoes it, it shall be expiation for him. And whoever judges not by what Allah has revealed, those are the wrongdoers.

5:46 And **We sent after them in their footsteps Jesus,** son of Mary, **verifying that which was before him of the Torah**; and We gave him **the Gospel containing guidance and light, and verifying that which was before it of the Torah**, and a guidance and an admonition for the dutiful.

Note: We are often reminded in the Qur'an that individuals are only responsible for their own deeds and thoughts. Why would Muhammad be guardian over the Torah and Gospel? The (only) logical answer is that Muhammad (as Moses) helped reveal the Torah, and though not physically present, helped with the ministry of Jesus.

5:48 And **We have revealed to thee the Book with the truth, verifying that which is before it of the Book and a guardian over it,** so judge between them by what Allah has revealed, and follow not their low desires, turning away from the truth that has come to thee. For every one of you We appointed a law and a way. And if Allah had pleased He would have made you a single people, but that He might try you in what He gave you. So vie one with another in virtuous deeds. To Allah you will all return, so He will inform you of that wherein you differed;

Chapter 6
Note: The following verses show that Moses as Muhammad is doing a repeat.

6:151 Say: Come! I will recite what your Lord has forbidden to you: Associate naught with Him and do good to parents and slay not your children for (fear of) poverty – We provide for you and for them – and draw not nigh to indecencies, open or secret, and kill not the soul which Allah has made sacred except in the course of justice. This He enjoins upon you that you may understand.

6:155 **Again, We gave the Book to Moses to complete (Our blessings) on him who would do good, and making plain all things and a guidance** and a mercy, so that they might believe in the meeting with their Lord.

6:155 **And this is a Book We have revealed, full of blessings; so follow it** and keep your duty that mercy may be shown to you,

6:157 **Lest you should say that the Book was revealed only to two parties** before us and We were truly unaware of what they read,

6:158 Or, **lest you should say: If the Book had been revealed to us, we would have been better guided than they. So indeed there has come to you clear proof from your Lord, and guidance and mercy.** Who is then more unjust than he who rejects Allah's messages and turns away from them? We reward those who turn away from Our messages with an evil chastisement because they turned away.

6:165 Say: Shall I seek a Lord other than Allah, while He is the Lord of all things? And no soul earns (evil) but against itself. **Nor does a bearer of burden bear the burden of another.** Then to your Lord is your return, so He will inform you of that in which you differed.

Chapter 7
7:6 Then certainly **We shall question those to whom messengers were sent, and We shall question the messengers,**

7:35 O children of Adam, **if messengers come to you from among you relating to you** My messages, then whosoever guards against evil and acts right– they shall have no fear, nor shall they grieve.

7:36 But those who reject Our Ayât (proofs, evidences, verses, lessons, signs, revelations, etc.) and treat them with arrogance, they are the dwellers of the (Hell) Fire, they will abide therein forever.

7:37 **Who is more unjust than one who invents a lie against Allâh or rejects His messages?** For such their appointed portion will reach them from the Book (of Decrees) until, when Our Messengers (the angel of death and his assistants) come to them to take their souls, they (the angels) will say: "Where are those whom you used to invoke and worship besides Allâh," they will reply, "They have vanished and deserted us." And they will bear witness against themselves, that they were disbelievers.

7:53 Do they wait for aught but its **final sequel?** On the day when its final sequel comes, those who neglected it before will say: Indeed the messengers of our Lord brought the truth. Are there any intercessors on our behalf so that they should intercede for us? **Or could we be sent back** so that we should do (deeds) other than those which we did? Indeed they have lost their souls, and that which they forged has failed them.

Note: Below: Who is mentioned in the Torah, Gospel, and Qur'an? Who could this be but Moses? And The revelation (Khalim's vision) confirms it.

7:157 Those who follow **the Messenger-Prophet, the Ummi (one who neither reads nor writes), whom they find mentioned in the Torah and the Gospel.** He enjoins them good and forbids them evil, and makes lawful to them the good things and prohibits for them impure things, and removes from them their burden and the shackles which were on them. So those who believe in him and honor him and help him, and follow the light which has been sent down with him – these are the successful.

7:158 Say: O mankind, surely **I am the Messenger of Allah to you all, of Him, Whose is the kingdom of the heavens and the earth.** There is no god but He; **He gives life and causes death.** So believe in Allah and His Messenger, the Ummi Prophet who believes in Allah and His words, and follow him so that you may be guided right.

Chapter 9

9:30 And **the Jews say: 'Uzair (Ezra) is the son of Allâh, and the Christians say: Messiah is the son of Allâh.** That is a saying from their mouths. They imitate the saying of the disbelievers of old. Allâh's Curse be on them, how they are deluded away from the truth!

9:33 It is He Who has sent His Messenger with guidance and the religion of truth (Islâm), that He may **make it to prevail over all religions** even though the Mushrikûn (polytheists, pagans, idolaters, disbelievers in the Oneness of Allâh) hate it.

34

Chapter 10

10:47 And **for every Ummah (a community or a nation), there is a Messenger;** when their Messenger comes, the matter will be judged between them with justice, and they will not be wronged.

10:48 And they say: "When will be this promise (the torment or the Day of Resurrection), - if you speak the truth?"

10:49 Say: "I have no power over any harm or profit to myself except what Allâh may will. **For every Ummah (a community or a nation), there is a term appointed; when their term is reached, neither can they delay it nor can they advance it an hour** (or a moment)."

Chapter 14

14:4 And **We sent not a Messenger except with the language of his people, in order that he might make the Message clear for them.** Then Allâh misleads whom He wills and guides whom He wills. And He is the All-Mighty, the All-Wise.

Chapter 16

16:101 And when **We change a verse in place of another**, and Allâh knows the best of what He sends down, they say: "You are but a Muftari! (forger, liar)." Nay, but most of them know not.

Chapter 17

17:13 And **We have fastened every man's deeds to his neck**, and on the Day of Resurrection, We shall bring out for him a book which he will find wide open.

17:14 (It will be said to him): "Read your book. You yourself are sufficient as a reckoner against you this Day."

17:15 **Whoever goes right, then he goes right only for the benefit of his own self.** And whoever goes astray, then he goes astray to his own loss. No one laden with burdens can bear another's burden. And We never punish until We have sent a Messenger to give warning.

17:16 And when We decide to destroy a town (population), We (first) send a definite order (to obey Allâh and be righteous) to those among them, or We (first) increase in number those of its population who are given the good things of this life. Then, they transgress therein, and thus the word is justified against it (them). Then We destroy it with complete destruction.

17:77 This was **Our Sunnah (rule) with the Messengers We sent before you, and you will not find any alteration in Our way.**

Chapter 20   35

20:36: He said: Thou art indeed granted thy petition, O Moses.

20:37 And indeed **We bestowed on thee a favor at another time,**

20:38 **When we revealed to thy mother that which was revealed** (i.e., to put Moses in a basket and put the basket into the river).

Chapter 22

22:78 And strive hard in Allâh's Cause as you ought to strive. **He has chosen you, and has not laid upon you in religion any hardship**, it is the religion of your father Abraham. It is He (Allâh) Who **has named you Muslims both before and in this (the Qur'ân)**, that the Messenger may be a witness over you and you be witnesses over mankind! So perform As– Salât (Iqamat-as-Salât), give Zakât and hold fast to Allâh. He is your Maula (Patron, Lord, etc.), what an Excellent Lord, and what an Excellent Helper!

Chapter 23

23:91 No son (or offspring or children) did Allâh beget, nor is there any ilâh (god) along with Him; (if there had been many gods), behold, each god would have taken away what he had created, and some would have tried to overcome others! Glorified be Allâh above all that they attribute to Him!

Chapter 27
27:75 And there is **nothing hidden in the heaven and the earth, but is in a Clear Book** (i.e., Al-Lauh Al-Mahfûz).

Note: Don't those who see, think, and reflect realize that the Qur'an is mostly about the Jews and their ancestors that are mentioned in the Torah and Gospel?

27:76 **Verily, this Qur'ân narrates to the Children of Israel most of that about which they differ.**
27:77 And truly, **it (this Qur'ân) is a guide and a mercy to the believers.**
33:56 **Allâh sends His Salât (Graces, Honors, Blessings, Mercy, etc.) on the Prophet, and also His angels too ask Allâh to bless and forgive him.** O you who believe! Send your Salât on him, and greet him with the Islâmic way of greeting (salutation i.e. As–Salâmu 'Alaikum).

Chapter 40
40:34 And indeed **Yûsuf (Joseph) did come to you, in times gone by, with clear signs,** but you ceased not to doubt in that which he did bring to you, till when he died you said: "**No Messenger will Allâh send after him.**" Thus Allâh leaves astray him who is a Musrif (a polytheist, oppressor, a criminal, sinner who commit great sins) and a Murtâb (one who doubts Allâh's Warning and His Oneness).

40:35 **Those who dispute about the messages of Allâh, without any authority that has come to them, it is greatly hateful and disgusting to Allâh and to those who believe.** Thus does Allâh seal up the heart of every arrogant, tyrant.

Chapter 42
Note: See below: We will follow in Muhammad's footsteps and call for the Unity of Judaism, Christianity, and Islam.

42:13 **Allâh has made plain to you the religion (Islâm) which He enjoined upon Nûh (Noah), and that which We revealed to you (Muhammad), and which We enjoined on Ibrahîm (Abraham), Mûsa (Moses), and Jesus - to establish religion, and not be divided therein.** Intolerable for the Mushrikûn (polytheists), is that to which you call them. Allâh chooses for Himself whom He wills, and guides unto Himself who turns to Him in repentance and in obedience.

42:14 **And they were not divided until after knowledge had come to them, out of envy among themselves.** And had not a Word gone forth from your Lord for an appointed term, the matter would have been settled between them. And verily, those who were made to inherit the Scripture after them are in grave doubt concerning it.

42:15 **To this then go on inviting, and be steadfast as you are commanded,** and follow not their desires but say: "I believe in whatsoever Allâh has sent down of the Book [all the holy Books, this Qur'ân and the Books of the old from the Taurât (Torah), or the Injeel (Gospel) or the Pages of Ibrâhim (Abraham)] and **I am commanded to do justice among you, Allâh is our Lord and your Lord. For us our deeds and for you your deeds. There is no dispute between us and you.** Allâh will gather us together, and to Him is the final return.

42:51 **It is not given to any human being that Allâh should speak to him unless (it be) by Inspiration, or from behind a veil, or (that) He sends a Messenger to reveal what He wills by His Leave.** Verily, He is Most High, Most Wise.
Chapter 43
43:31 And they say: **"Why is not this Qur'ân sent down to some great man of the two towns (Makkah and Tâ'if)?"**

43:52 **"Am I not better than this Moses, who is Mahîn [has no honor nor any respect, and is weak and despicable] and can scarcely express himself clearly?**

43:53 "Why then are not golden bracelets bestowed on him, or angels sent along with him?"

43:54 Thus Pharaoh fooled and misled his people, and they obeyed him. Verily, they were ever a people who were Fâsiqûn (rebellious, disobedient to Allâh).

43:55 **So when they angered Us, We punished them, and drowned them all.**

43:56 And We made them a precedent (as a lesson for those coming after them), and an example to later generations.

43:59 He (Jesus) was not more than a servant. We granted Our Favor to him, and We made him an example to the Children of Israel.

43:61 And **Jesus, son of Mary shall be a known sign for the coming of the Hour (Day of Resurrection).** Therefore have no doubt concerning it (i.e., the Day of Resurrection). And follow Me (Allâh) ! This is the Straight Path.

43:63 And when 'Iesa (Jesus) came with (Our) clear Proofs, he said: **"I have come to you with Al-Hikmah (Prophethood), and in order to make clear to you some of the (points) in which you differ, therefore fear Allâh and obey me,**

43:64 "Verily, Allâh! He is my Lord (God) and your Lord (God). **So worship Him. (Alone).** This is the (only) Straight Path."

43:65 But the sects from among themselves differed. So woe to those who do wrong (by ascribing things to 'Iesa (Jesus) that are not true from the torment of a painful Day (i.e., the Day of Resurrection)!

Chapter 44

44:14 Then they had turned away from him (Messenger Muhammad) and said: **"One taught (by a human being), madman!"**

44:17 And indeed We tried before them Pharaoh's people, when **there came to them a noble Messenger (Moses),**

44:18 Saying: **"Restore to me the servants of Allâh (the Children of Israel). Verily! I am to you a Messenger worthy of all trust,**

44:19 "And exalt not (yourselves) against Allâh. Truly, **I have come to you with a manifest authority.**

44:56 **In Paradise, they will never taste death therein except the first death** (of this world), and He will save them from the torment of the blazing Fire,

Chapter 46

46:9 Say: **"I am not a new thing among the Messengers (of Allâh)** nor do I know what will be done with me or with you. I only follow that which is revealed to me, and I am but a plain warner."

46:10 Say: "Tell me! **If this Qur'ân is from Allâh, and you deny it, and a witness from among the Children of Israel ('Abdullâh bin Salâm radhiallahu'anhu) has borne witness of one like him** (Prophet Muhammad), so he believed, then why are you so big with pride?" Verily! Allâh guides not the people who are disbelievers and wrongdoers.

46:11 And those who disbelieve (strong and wealthy) say of those who believe (weak and poor): **"Had it been a good thing, they (the weak and poor) would not have preceded us thereto!"** And when they have not let themselves be guided by it (this Qur'ân), they say: "This is an ancient lie!"

Note: See Below. Who could confirm it better than its earthly co-originator, Moses?

46:12: And **before this was the Scripture of Moses as a guide and a mercy. And this is a confirming Book** in the Arabic language, to warn those who do wrong, and as glad tidings to the Muhsinûn (good-doers - see V. 2:112).

Chapter 48

48:28 He it is Who has sent His Messenger with guidance and the religion of truth, that He may make it **prevail over all religions.** And All-Sufficient is Allâh as a Witness.

48:29 Muhammad is the Messenger of Allâh, and those who are with him are firm against disbelievers, and merciful among themselves. You see them bowing and falling down prostrate (in prayer), seeking Bounty from Allâh and (His) Good Pleasure. The mark of them (of their Faith) is on their faces (fore- heads) from the traces of their prostration (during prayers). **This is their description in the Torah. But their description in the Gospel** is like a seed which sends forth its shoot, then makes it strong, it then becomes thick, and it stands straight on its stem, delighting the sowers that He may enrage the disbelievers with them. Allâh has promised those among them who believe and do righteous good deeds, forgiveness and a mighty reward.

Chapter 53

Note: Because he is the Reincarnation of Moses, ...

53:56 **Muhammad is a warner (Messenger) of the series of warners of old.**

Chapter 57
57:26 And indeed, **We sent Nûh (Noah) and Ibrahîm (Abraham), and placed in their offspring Prophethood and Scripture,** and among them there is he who is guided, but many of them are Fâsiqûn (rebellious, disobedient to Allâh).
57:27 Then, We sent after them, Our Messengers, and We sent Jesus – son of Maryam (Mary), and gave him the Injeel (Gospel). And We ordained in the hearts of those who followed him, compassion and mercy. But the Monasticism which they invented for themselves, We did not prescribe for them, but (they sought it) only to please Allâh therewith, but that they did not observe it with the right observance. So We gave those among them who believed, their (due) reward, but many of them are Fâsiqûn (rebellious, disobedient to Allâh).

Note: See below. Why would you get a double portion?

57:28 **O you who believe in Moses (the Jews) and Jesus (the Christians)! Fear Allâh, and believe too in His Messenger Muhammad, He will give you a double portion** of His Mercy, and He will give you a light by which you shall walk straight, and He will forgive you. And Allâh is Oft-Forgiving, Most Merciful.

Chapter 61

61:6 And remember when **Jesus, son of Maryam, said: "O Children of Israel! I am the Messenger of Allâh unto you confirming the Torah before me, and giving glad tidings of a Messenger to come after me, whose name shall be Ahmed.** But when he (Ahmed) came to them with clear proofs, they said: "This is plain magic."

61:9 He it is Who has sent His Messenger with guidance and the religion of truth to **make it prevail over all religions** even though the Mushrikûn disbelievers hate it.

Chapter 66

69:11 Verily! **When the water rose beyond its limits, We carried you in the floating ship that was constructed by Noah.**

Chapter 72

72:27 **Except to a Messenger (from mankind) whom He has chosen (He informs him of unseen as much as He likes), and then He makes a band of watching guards (angels) to march before him and behind him.**

72:28 **Allâh protects them (the Messengers), till He sees that they (the Messengers) have conveyed the Messages of their Lord (Allâh).** And He (Allâh) surrounds all that which is with them, and He (Allâh) keeps count of all things.

13 SAD CONDITION: THE MIDDLE EAST LEADERS

Doesn't it seem mighty strange to see the oppression, degradation, and violence against the Palestinians while "leaders" like Hosni Mubarak, the Saudi's, Jordanians, Turks, Indonesians, Kuwaiti's, etc. stand by, doing nothing decisive about it, sometimes complicit in it.

Imperial USA Policies

The USA has become what it fought against in 1776, 1812, 1917, and 1941. This is not good. It is not right. There will be a day of reckoning.

The State of Israel

We sometimes ask, "What would Jesus do?"

What would Jesus do about the Zionist State of Israel? Its very existence violates international norms. You can't go and take someone else's property (their land) because you have a bigger and better gun (in 1948) - and have it stand! Jesus would look at its existence, its policies, its violence against, and conduct toward the Palestinians, its exceptionalism. He would note what happened to it before, when it wrought evil, injustice, oppression, murder, and other evil acts against other human beings (and God's prophets). He would note the reason for its EXPULSION from Palestine in about 70 A.D. - and at previous times. He might note that people who support what it does are said by John to have "The Mark of the Beast!" He would likely predict another EXPULSION! He also might note how it eggs the United States on - to do evil, unjust, and immoral things.

He might even note how many of those who support it violate, and encourage the violation of the Laws of Moses, Jesus, and Prophet Muhammad relative to homosexuality and usury.

Miscellaneous: Eating Contests; Misrepresenting "Black"

It makes my blood boil to see people on TV gulping down food like dogs (or some other starving animal), as fast as they can, in some kind of eating contest.

The Anchors on TV smile, grin, and are so happy to show you and tell you about this vulgar, obscene, and wicked display of people behaving in a manner lower than beasts!

Not only that, but in the meantime, there are people (many people) all over the world, STARVING!

Many commentators on TV, radio, or elsewhere often speak of Serial Killers, murderers, charlatans, events, (days), or even a kind of humor as "dark or black." Somehow, "white" Adolph Hitler becomes "dark."

First, most seem to have no idea of how "color" works. When you add more colors to light, you finally get "white" light. When you add more color (or pigment) to matter, you get darker and darker colors.

I love blackness. "Dark" thunderstorms are an awesome display in nature, and give life and nourishment. I love to go into deep, black, restful sleep. I love to contemplate in the quiet, still blackness. I love the blackness of the skin, and all the colors of the skin. Darker pigments of the skin show that one's biological ancestors got a lot of sun. The relative absence indicates that one's biological ancestors received less sunlight!

The abundance of life and energy emanates from the sun, creating darker colors. We should celebrate and use this energy - and view "Black" as positive and abundant life and energy. We go into the "blackness" to get sleep, rest, and to get recharged!

What the Commentators really mean is that these diabolical characters, Serial Killers, for example, are acting very "white" - if you would assign a "color" to it. The lying, murderous, war-mongering George W. Bush acts very "white!" George W. Bush leans to the Rome/Greece, beastly side of America - not the Jeffersonian/Jacobian good-side.

The USA is Israel

The USA is the real Israel, for it was established under the Covenant of The Declaration of Independence and Thomas Jefferson. He was instrumental in getting the Bill of Rights and other safeguards included in the US Constitution.

Jefferson is the reincarnated Jacob, father of the 12 boys, who over time, became known as Israel. This is why the USA has been blessed and guarded - up to a point!

So, the US has a split personality, if you will. It has a good side, and it has an evil, or bad side. It is part Rome and Greece. So, it has an inherent inclination to empire, brutality, and war. The Rome/Greece side can also be seen in its excesses, in the "lie, cheat, steal, and deny responsibility" tendencies - and in slavery. The corrupt Congress and homosexuality may come out of the "Rome/Greece DNA."

But Ancient Israel was also part good, and part bad. We must now separate the good from the bad, and remove that bad Rome/Greece DNA!

The Zionist Entity in the Middle East is NOT legitimate Israel. In fact, where is the good side? That leadership there, European immigrants, seem to be all Rome/Greece - Crusaders, war-mongers, unfair, unjust, racist, violent, destroyers!

The USA supports the Zionist Entity (in part) because it "feels" that "someone is Israel!" It should look in the mirror!

The Zionist Entity should melt (integrate itself) into a Middle East (without its current borders). They are no different than anybody else. We cannot have a State that is ethnically or religiously cleansed!

13 THE REBIRTH OF THE USA

There will be a rebirth in America (the USA) and the world, but it requires work. It requires right knowledge and right actions, truthfulness- and working for God, and with God, to do the work that needs to be done.

We must operate within righteousness, and this means that we must know right from wrong, and act accordingly.

I will list some actions we will propose.

First though, it is interesting to note that this country is in many ways similar to ancient Israel- in its goodness, and in its evil. And I will not get into many of the comparisons at this time, but I do want you to look at a comparison of the cycle of the Hebrew nation's kings with the cycle of presidents of the USA:

1. Abraham, Gen. 11:26	George Washington, 1789
2. Isaac, Gen. 21:2	John Adams, 1797
3. Jacob (Israel), Gen. 25:26	Thomas Jefferson, 1801
4. Judas, Gen. 29:35	James Madison, 1809
5. Phares, Gen. 46:12	James Monroe, 1817
6. Esrom, Gen. 46:12	John Quincy Adams, 1825
7. Aram, Ruth 4:19	Andrew Jackson, 1829
8. Aminadab. Num. 1:7	Martin van Buren, 1837
9. Nasson, Num. 1:7	William I. Harrison, 1841
10. Salmon, Ruth 4:20	John Tyler, 1841
11. Booz, Ruth 4:21	James K. Polk 1845
12. Obed, Ruth 4:17	Zachary Taylor, 1849
13. Jesse, Ruth 4:22	Millard Fillmore, 1850
14. David, 1 Chron. 2:15	Franklin Pierce, 1853
15. Solomon, 2 Samuel 12:24	James Buchanan, 1857
16. Roboam, 1 Kings 11:43	Abraham Lincoln, 1861
17. Abia, 1 Kings 15:1	Andrew Johnson, 1865
18. Asa, 1 Kings 15:9	Ulysses S. Grant, 1869
19. Josaphat, 22:41	Rutherford B. Hayes, 1877
20. Joram, 2 Kings 8:16	James Abram Garfield, 1881
21. Ozias, 2 Kings 8:25	Chester A. Authur 1881
22. Joatham, 2 Kings 15:32	Grover Cleveland, 1885
23. Achaz, 2 Kings 16:1	Benjamin Harrison 1889
24. Ezekias, 2 Kings 18:1	Grover Cleveland, 1893
25. Manasses, 2 Kings 21:1	William McKinley, 1897
26. Amon, 2 Kings 21:18	Theodore Roosevelt, 1901
27. Josias, 2 Kings 21:24	William H. Taft, 1909
28. Jechonias 1 Chron. 3:16	Woodrow Wilson, 1913
29. Salathiel, 1 Chron. 3:17	Warren G. Harding, 1921

30. Zorobabel, 1 Chron. 3:19	Calvin Coolidge, 1923
31. Abiud, (Matthew)	Herbert C. Hoover, 1929
32. Eliakim, (Matthew)	F. D. Roosevelt, 1933
33. Azor, (Matthew)	Harry S. Truman, 1945
34. Sadoc, (Matthew)	Dwight D. Eisenhower, 1953
35. Achim, (Matthew)	John F. Kennedy, 1961
36. Elind, (Matthew)	Lyndon B. Johnson, 1963
37. Eleazar, (Matthew)	Richard M. Nixon, 1969
38. Matthan, (Matthew)	Gerald R. Ford, 1974
39. Jacob, (Matthew)	Jimmy Carter, 1977
40. Joseph, (Jesus' father)	Ronald Wilson Reagan, 1981
41. Jesus, (Matthew)	George H. W. Bush, 1989
42. Christ, (Matthew)	William Jefferson Clinton, 1993
43. None; covenant over	George W. Bush, 2001
44. None; covenant over	Barack Obama, 2009

Very often the comparisons show the very similar, or very opposite. Some of the comparisons are listed below:

1. Abraham, and George Washington moved away from their nations and started new nations. Washington was a warrior; Abraham fought against Chedorlaomer (Gen. 14:5).

3. Jacob (Israel) is the father, through his offspring, of the Hebrew nation and the West. Jefferson is the father of the ideals of the USA.

14. Franklin Pierce became the youngest President of his time. He hastened the Civil War by signing the Kansas-Nebraska Act of 1854. David was a young warrior, and the best in his character was the opposite to that of Pierce's.

15. Solomon was wise, and had about 1000 wives. James Buchanan is considered one of the worst presidents because of his lack of judgment and moral courage, and the only bachelor President.

16. Abraham Lincoln saved the Union and is considered a moral individual. His counterpart, Roboam, presided over the breakup of the Jewish state into Judah, and Israel. Roboam was immoral. **Barack Obama is the reincarnation of Abraham Lincoln.**

28. Woodrow Wilson was a good man. His counterpart, Jechonias was a scoundrel.

30. Calvin Coolidge said the business of America is business. Salathiel, the counterpart said the business of Israel was justice and righteousness.

39. Jacob, of course is another word which means James, Jimmy, Israel; and it means "he who would provide service to his fellow man." So, Jimmy Carter works for "Habitat," an organization which provides service from man to his fellow man.

40. Joseph (Jesus' "father") helped to prepare a channel that became the hope of humanity. The world is forever indebted to him. He went to Egypt to avoid death to his son. The counterpart, Ronald Reagan, presided over the USA becoming the world's biggest debtor nation.

Also, the national debt went from $1 trillion to 3 trillion. Reagan invaded tiny Grenada, and bullied other small nations. He also said things that had little or no resemblance to facts. MANY USA CITIZENS JUST LOVED Reagan!

41, 42. Note: Jesus was oppressed and escaped to Egypt to save his young life. As the Christ, he made a way for many, to save many lives...

To tell the truth,   To be of service,
To heal the sick   To feed the hungry To give man hope
To lift the oppressed To free the captives
To comfort the weary
To encourage those who fight against evil
TO LEAD MAN BACK TO HIS FINAL DESTINATION!

Bush, the counterpart, invaded Panama. He killed the children, and women, and men in his way. He murdered tens of thousands of children, women, and men in Iraq. The USA citizens loved it. Jesus the oppressed, Bush, the oppressor! Opposites!

So, you can see by many indications that this country has a lot of good, and ultra-bad mixed in together. And yes, it has been rightly called the head of the Great Satan because of its past, even current, leaders. But it is changing, and it will become a place that God Himself will be proud of.

But we must do what is right, because only right makes might, and this is what we will do:

- We will unfreeze the assets of other countries (Iran, etc.) because we must undo unjust acts. And we must treat others like we want to be treated.

- So-called affirmative action will become a dead issue because of Jubilee and bartering (and righteousness). Remember, God is not a respecter of ethnicity, gender, or nationality. And we are made in His image.

And we like he, are One. And we will all work together. And leadership will be in sharing of skills, knowledge, and resources.

And God is always watching what you do.

- Much testing will take place to identify potential leaders, and potential problems.

And we know what the norms are. And we know what the characteristics of devils are. For, foremost with them are selfishness, envy, greed, lies, hatred, phoniness, backstabbing, and ignorance.

We will take the evil nose of the government, and the media, out of people's bedrooms. Some things should be private. And I wonder how many inheritors of The Tradition know about the lives of Abraham, Jacob, King David, Solomon, Muhammad, etc. Also, as I said earlier, abortion is a private matter. And God will reward or punish you for what you do (or don't do).

The Israeli State will he found to be unjust. And it is a big mess. We are all JEWS (real Jews)- when we join in completing the Spiritual Revolution that brings about the completion of the Cycle of Judaism, and that brings about the Second Coming. And we are witnessing that.

A peaceful resolution is the best solution. And remember, Abraham had two sons, and they were and are dear to him. The "sibling rivalry" must not go too far. And we will have our place in the New World, for all of our needs will be filled, and those who overstep the limits will go to hell.

So Egypt and others will be key players. And Israel can turn into a coordinator which provides many of the needs of the people in the area.

So, in closing, also remember, all God's souls are legal. Don't call souls illegitimate. Remember how Jesus was conceived. Don't use ignorant words like minority. We are all major-in God. And never, never say you are the devil's advocate, etc.

AND WE EXECUTE JUBILEE in the name of the God of Israel. And the precedent is the Law of God, as handed down through Moses and Muhammad.

THE EMANCIPATION PROCLAMATION is also a precedent..

And God will certainly execute his will.

And there must be the will, on the part of God's Chosen to remove from the earth those who came here a long time ago to fill the earth with much evil.

John saw the devils coming. In Revelation 12:7, he says, "And there was war in heaven: Michael and his angels fought against the dragon; and the dragon fought and his angels, And prevailed not; neither was their place found any more in heaven. And the great dragon was cast out, that old serpent, called the Devil, and Satan, which deceiveth the whole world: he was cast out into the earth, and his angels were cast out with him. And I heard a loud voice saying in heaven, Now is come salvation, and strength, and the kingdom of our God, and the power of his Christ: for the accuser of our brethren is cast down, which accused them before our God day and night. And they overcame him by the blood of the Lamb, and by the word of their testimony; and they loved not their lives unto the death. Therefore rejoice, ye heavens, and ye that dwell in them. Woe to the inhibiters of the earth and of the sea! For, the devil is come down unto you, having great wrath, because he hath but a short time."

AND NOW HIS TIME IS UP ON EARTH TOO! And the accusers will be bound in the bowels of hell 1000 years!

For, we will attack them! We will attack them with truth! We will attack them with unity! We will attack them with brotherhood! We will attack them with sharing and caring! We will attack them with cooperation! We will attack them with patience and moderation!

JIHAD! JIHAD! ATTACK! ATTACK!

WE WILL ATTACK THEM NONVIOLENTLY, WITH THE FULL FORCE OF SOUL POWER!

When they are negative and morbid, we will be positive and optimistic. Where they see only ugliness, we will see beauty and balance.

When they seek to accuse us unjustly, we will seek out their lies, and relentlessly beat them with their lies!

When they come to us with their half-truths, we will note that they store lies in one part of their brain, and facts in another, and therefore they speak with forked tongues. Therefore, for instance, the devils will tell you government doesn't create jobs. Yet, there are about 20 million directly employed by government, including many accusers.

So, when the devils come to you to accuse their brethren, tell them, "You know, the United People are right. We really are our brother's keeper. And I cannot find any fault with this man." When they come to you touting the "very fine" laws of the Great Satan, say, "Where was the Supreme Court when

African Americans virtually had no rights?" Say, "Even the pagan, barbaric societies knew you must have a god- the real thing, or a substitute for Him." Say, "The Congress, and the courts don't understand fundamentals." Therefore issues, and problems, like abortion, freedom of the press (the media), garbage (talk) radio, and talk shows; welfare, government debt, education, crime, unemployment, etc., arise, or are created by them.

Then, they sit around on their fat bottoms and pass more and more laws, and collect more and more taxes. And things get worse and worse.

Look at the ones running for president in 1992: Graham, Lugar, Clinton, etc. Most of them are the architects, or the fellow-travelers of the architects of the bankruptcy, and failed policies that have led to the general collapse of the society.

So, we must move up. Unite. Create the Jubilee Party, of United People, of the United States.

Be the opposite of those devils:

Confound the accusers with courage and caution
Defeat them with devotion and loyalty to God and man
Overcome their lies with love, faith, and trust in God
And greet their hopelessness with your winning smile!

And let's be about our Father's Business

For, my fellow Americans
"We implement the Millennium
With Jesus, Moses, and Muhammad at our side
God's will becomes our own
And we will love and help our Second Israel...

51

Tell the truth
Prophesy, philosophy
Expel the devils from our land... My love for you is boundless

And I am always at your side... in flesh, or spirit"

And the trumpet of God is sounding throughout the land!

And we proclaim liberty to all the inhabitants thereof.

SING:

"FREE AT LAST

FREE AT LAST

THANK GOD, ALMIGHTY WE'RE FREE, AT LAST!"

14 JUBILEE WORLDWIDE NOW!

After the 2012 Election (in the USA), chop 25% off the USA and world debt (worldwide). Eliminate the $1 trillion USA student loan debt! The USA is Israel! This is the Millennium, the Resurrection! Good people and God's Chosen lead the way.

In 2013, chop ANOTHER 25% off the USA and world debt (worldwide). This is the era of the Second Coming! In 2014, chop ANOTHER 25% off the USA and world debt (worldwide).

New Rules
1. Make it where you sell it. Production must take place where the products are sold – as much as possible.
2. CEO pay should be no more than 1-4 times that of the average worker.
3. Moses and Prophet Muhammad (the same soul) forbade charging "interest" as practiced in the USA (and the West). The immoral (sinful) application must be stopped.
4. Everyone must work or be allowed to work. Everyone can and will contribute - as decreed in the Scriptures (Acts: 2:44-45; 4:32, 35). Use the Amish, the early Christians, et.al. as examples(models) of this concept.
5. Penalize followers of Satan heavily! Rush Limbaugh, FOX NEWS, and the Republican/Tea Party lie, cheat and steal. They are serial, pathological liars, living in their own insular, delusional worlds. When they lie, make them pay!
6. God resides in you – unless the devil resides in you. We can tell who resides in you - by what you say and do. If God resides in you, then you will help us establish God's heaven-on-earth.
7. People without integrity, habitual liars - like Mitt Romney, Rush Limbaugh, Sean Hannity, Donald Trump, Bill O'Reilly, Sarah Palin, Jerome Corsi, Joe Arpaio, Dinesh D'Souza, Karl Rove, Gov. Rick Scott, Herman Cain, Hank Williams Jr., Newt Gingrich, and John Sununu are devils. They belong in hell.
8. Jubilee Worldwide! Establish Jubilee Worldwide over the next four years – or ASAP. The current economic system has been rigged against many people over the last 30 to 50 years. For some it has been stacked against them for 400-500 years.
9. Money is just a means of exchange for "bartering." You cannot eat, use as shelter, or clothe yourself in money or gold. Focus on the

goods or services that must be distributed - justly and morally. Just distribution recognizes that you only have one stomach, and just two feet, two hands and one body.

Modern technology, robotics, and machines have made much of the work previously done by humans a thing of the past. Production is so high and efficient that the labor force participation rate today is at 63.5 percent in the USA: a 31-year low. ***Work must be shared.***

The old Economics does not work in our advanced societies, in the Resurrection.

Society must be structured to serve the people; people are not here to serve a dysfunctional, unjust, and immoral society. Example: We must alter or abolish the US Supreme Court and the US Congress.

Jubilee: Leviticus 25:8-13 says, "And thou shall number 7-Sabbaths of years unto thee, 7 times 7 years; and the space of 7 Sabbaths of years shall be unto thee 40 and 9 years. Then shalt thou cause the trumpet of the Jubilee to sound on the 10th day of the 7th month, in the Day of Atonement shall ye make the trumpet sound throughout the land. And ye shall hallow the fiftieth year, and proclaim liberty throughout all the land unto all the inhabitants thereof: it shall be a Jubilee unto you. And ye shall return every man unto his possession, and ye shall return every man unto his family."

Jubilee will cancel (or reset) all debt, including federal, state, local, business, farm, individual, student, family, and international. All countries, like the USA, Greece, Portugal, Ireland, Russia, Poland, Mexico, Nigeria, Brazil, Zaire, Canada, etc. become completely free of debt.
Precedents:

- The Emancipation Proclamation
- The Louisiana Purchase
- The colonization/acquisition of the United States
- Reparations payments to the State of Israel
- Reparations payments to Japanese Americans who were wrongfully incarcerated in the USA
- Infrastructure, employment, and construction programs (of the CCC and the WPA) under President Franklin D. Roosevelt
- Jubilee implementation under ancient Israel

Thomas Jefferson is the reincarnation of Jacob (aka Israel). The USA *is* Israel. Prophet Muhammad is the reincarnation of Moses. Barack Obama is the reincarnation of Abraham Lincoln. I am a witness. (Genesis 32:28-29, 35:10). Judaism, Christianity, and Islam are *one* faith. We are *one* people.

This is the Millennium, the Resurrection! Good people and God's Chosen lead the way.

16 INDEX

16 ABOUT THE AUTHOR, AND OTHER BOOKS

Youssef Khalim obtained Unity in yoga on about 7/20/80. He says, "We will recombine into one faith, Judaism, Christianity, and Islam." He has been able to "see" and experience some amazing information about USA presidents Jefferson, Lincoln, and Obama; and also Prophets Moses, Muhammad, and Solomon - in visions, lucid dreams, and in meditation. Khalim makes reincarnation (resurrection) central again in our western religions. He resides in the Chicagoland area. And he is the father of Tonya, Runako, and Noah. See his books on the following websites: http://lulu.com, http://amazon.com, and http://sunracommunications.com

OTHER BOOKS

Youssef Khalim's books include *People Of The Future/Day; You Are Too Beautiful; I Love You Back; You Look So Good; The Resurrection Of Noah; Healing Begins With The Mind; Jubilee Worldwide; Galina, All About Love; Ekaterina, Hot and Lovely; Natalia, With Love; Svetlana, Angel Of Love; Lori, My Dream Girl; I Call My Sugar, Candie; Love of My Life*; and *The Second Coming!*